How to be an effective school governor

by Joan Sallis

Contents

Chapter 1 — 3
What part do governors play in schools?

Why do schools have governors? The part governors play. What DON'T governors do?: the headteacher's role. Common mistakes. What is meant by a 'strategic role'? Learning to find the right buttons and levers. Shall I ever be able to manage the job?

Chapter 2 — 10
Governing bodies and how they work

How are governing bodies composed? How do governing bodies work? The different kinds of governors. Meetings, committees and business – the role of the chair, confidentiality, minutes, committees etc.

Chapter 3 — 16
What are governors' responsibilities?

Someone like you can do it. Aims of the school, budget, staffing, curriculum, personnel management, pupils, premises, communication, informing parents, admissions, inspection.

Chapter 4 — 25
How to be a good representative

Understanding community needs. Representing parents. Dealing with individual concerns. Teacher governors and their role.

continued over page

Chapter 5 31
Being an effective member of a team

What makes a good team? Common purpose, loyalty, importance of training and experience, looking after weaker members, keeping to the rules, high expectations and shaming the slackers, accepting responsibility. The effective governor at the meeting. Tips and tactics. Being effective round and about. The good ambassador. Relations with the headteacher.

Appendix A 38
The composition of governing bodies

Appendix B 40
The different kinds of schools and their governing bodies

Appendix C 41
Rules and good practices for working together

Useful organisations 43

Further Reading 45

Published by the Advisory Centre for Education,
1B Aberdeen Studios, 22 Highbury Grove,
London N5 2DQ
© ACE1996
Designed by Richard and Sally Doust
Printed by College Hill Press
37 Webber Street, London SE1 8QW

ISBN 1870672 45 3

Joan Sallis is a member of the ACE Council, president of the Campaign for State Education, and a governor of a comprehensive school. She has written several guides for governors and the ACE Summaries of the Education Act 1986 and the 1988 Education Reform Act. She was a parent member of the Taylor committee which recommended many of the changes now incorporated in education law.

2 • © ACE 1996 Published by the ADVISORY CENTRE FOR EDUCATION

What Part do Governors Play in Schools?

Why do schools have governors?

When you became a school governor your first questions were probably "Why do schools have governors?" and "What does being a governor involve?" We hope this chapter will provide the answers.

Governors are not a new idea. Six hundred years ago the first recorded governing body was set up in a famous school – Winchester – which still exists. The tasks of those governors were not very different from yours today, even though schooling for everybody's children was not even dreamed of then. Nearly 500 years later in 1870, schooling became the right of all children and it was laid down that every school should have a group of locally appointed people to represent the public in the running of the school. This essentially is still the role of governors: to ensure that schools are run well and with due regard for those they serve, for every child has to receive schooling and every citizen helps pay for it. The quality of education also affects our lives in so many ways that everyone should be concerned about it.

So what's changed? Why are governors suddenly in the news and why were most people scarcely aware they existed before? Two things are different. One is that after a lot of campaigning by people who thought it was important, the law was altered in the 1980s to bring in parents, teachers and neighbours of the school itself to share this important task. Then, from 1988, schools gained much more freedom to run their affairs. Until then the local education authority (LEA) had helped choose the head and deputy, decided on the number of staff, paid the teachers, kept the school building in order, laid down the curriculum in broad outline, dealt with any staff misdemeanours, and generally watched the standard of work of the school. Each school was given just a small allowance of money to buy books, paper and other classroom necessities. All that has changed, as the next section shows.

Thus while governors still have the same basic function of looking after the interests of the ordinary people who use the school, the job has grown as the school has become self-managing. In effect governors now share in its management, a task more demanding but also vastly more interesting.

The part governors play

So governors are there to represent the community which the school serves. They are its eyes and ears in that neighbourhood and they bring a fresh perspective to the work of professional educators, a perspective from the streets, the workplaces, and the homes of that community. It is essential that schools remain in touch with those they serve and responsive to their needs. But governors are not just there to communicate. The governing body has a real part to play in shaping the school's policies, a chance to influence its development and on behalf of that community to advise, guide and warn as well as support the school in its work. It is also part of the governors' job to keep a watchful eye on the performance of the school, ensure that it is fair in its treatment of the people who work there, see that it respects parents' role in their children's education and is in every sense a good neighbour. Remember, however, that it is the governing body which has that responsibility, not the individual governor. You as an individual work always as part of a team.

The governing body's influence is at the strategic or policy-making level in the school. It shares in setting its aims, in planning for its future, and improving its performance. It decides broadly how the school budget should be spent, selects head and deputy, shares in policy-making for all aspects of the school's life and work, ensures that the premises are in good order, and sometimes settles disputes. It provides a watchful eye, an open ear and a steady hand in a crisis.

Governors' responsibilities are set out in more detail in Chapter 2.

What DON'T governors do?

Governors don't run the school day by day. It is a very unwise governor who attempts to do or duplicate the work of the paid staff. Most governors don't know how to teach fractions, set up an experiment, decide on the right text book or choose the best approach with a slow or difficult child. There are staff who will have had training (four years in the case of teachers) to do that and it would be silly to think untrained people with other jobs to do could improve on their efforts. Even if you happen to be a teacher yourself and do know the right way to do things, you haven't been employed to do them in that school. Even if teachers are doing something you know is wrong, it is the head's job to tell them, not you. Headteachers have been chosen to lead the staff and manage the enterprise because of exceptional ability and experience, and they are the ones whose jobs are on the line if they fail. They answer to us for the general effectiveness of the school and the performance of teachers. But they should share with governors all the strategic moves they plan to make.

The headteacher's role   The headteacher decides how best to spend the money governors approve under each general heading, how to use the staff and the space available, and how to manage the time in the school day. He or she leads the staff team and constantly seeks to improve their effectiveness. That means showing them, advising them, guiding them and, just now and then, telling them off. The head also sees to it that the school is an orderly place with an atmosphere that helps learning. That means dealing promptly and effectively with disruption from any cause. The head is the governors' chief professional adviser, obliged by law to give them the information they ask for to help them carry out their legal duties. He or she is also the school's chief public relations officer.

Grey areas   People often talk about 'grey areas' of responsibility, where heads and governors are in conflict. Very often these are responsibilities which it is quite easy to present as day-by-day management or delivery of the curriculum, but in which action is also quite likely to cause a great deal of commotion among parents. This turns them into responsibilities which heads ought to share with governors because they invade governors' communicating role. One good example is changing the age groupings in a primary school. Parents hate it and to be accepted it needs a lot of explanation. There are often good reasons, and although it is technically to do with the management of space and staff, it would be an unwise head who did not get governors' understanding first. In a secondary school, changing ability groupings raises similar issues. On curriculum delivery, the choice of methods of teaching reading could be said to be a professional concern. But again, changing a reading scheme is such a fundamental step for parents, who rightly see reading at the heart of their children's learning, that strong reactions are possible:

again it is wise to take the step in agreement with governors. A good principle is: if in doubt consult, especially in matters which may perturb parents or community.

Common mistakes When governors go wrong it is usually for one of two reasons. Either they forget that the responsibility belongs to the governing body as a whole and not individuals, or they get involved in too much detail. In the first category, well-meaning new governors may try to speak for the school or get too deeply into solving problems on their own. In the second category they check up on details of school organisation like the temperature of the classrooms or the punctuality of teachers. They may even behave like inspectors. A few will spend a lot of time just doing over again what someone in the school is paid to do – totalling up invoices, checking that equipment approved for purchase has actually been delivered, making sure the blocked basin has been cleared.

The strategic role It's often said that governors operate at the 'strategic level' in school affairs. It's not easy to define what that is – though you soon get to know what it isn't. For instance, it isn't desperately trying to find something penetrating to say about a lesson you have observed or worrying about the tens and units in every bit of school spending. It isn't championing the cause of all those parents who think their child ought to be on a higher reading book. It isn't constantly suggesting minor improvements. Nor is it related to the size of a problem. Rather, the 'strategic level' is defined by the nature of the action likely to contribute to its solution. That means learning just enough about how schools work to be able to visualise the 'control panel'. A school has its master controls just like an industrial plant or a power station, but they may be invisible. If a weakness appears in part of its work or a problem seems insoluble without radical re-thinking, asking the right questions is like finding those knobs and levers in the dark.

What does 'strategic' mean? It's worth spending some time on this idea of a strategic role, since governors often look puzzled when experts talk about the governing body's part in school improvement, or an aspect of the school's life or work which is causing concern. When governors get in trouble for 'meddling', it is often a well-meant response to not understanding what their role is – or understanding it and not being allowed to perform it.

A homely example might help. Just suppose you were the owner of a restaurant. During the early summer the staff always complain about the long time taken to scrape the new potatoes. You could say you'd go in daily yourself and help for an hour or so. You could go in and chivvy them along and see if you could get them to work more effectively. You could decide to pay them a seasonal bonus. You could decide to take on extra part-time staff for that period. Any of these things would help, but they are all decisions made within the old framework. Getting more strategic, you could invest in a machine which scraped potatoes just as though they'd been done by hand. Or you could instruct that they were boiled in their skins; lots of people do nowadays, and it's healthier. Or you could decide to serve a higher proportion of main dishes with rice or pasta for that period of the year. These might be called strategic decisions.

Look at levers A lever is a good thing to think about because it's a strategic instrument in a way that a hammer isn't. Although it's simple, it can lift amazing weights and enable the hand to command much more force than it could alone. (Probably your son or daughter still at school could express this in a formula.) Leverage is therefore a term often used in business to mean a process which enables the manager to find the simplest, if not the most obvious way, of making something happen.

In schools you can rarely solve serious problems or make big improvements without looking beyond those teachers in those classsrooms with those lessons. The levers may be the way you select or promote teachers, choose courses and learning materials, allot time for managing the teaching process and in-service training, group pupils, and organise all the built-in routines of motivating, checking, evaluating and chivvying.

Suppose your school had been inspected and the report slated the modern languages work in GCSE. You don't just get rid of all the teachers or even the faculty head! What questions do you ask? When did the problem begin? Had anything different happened that year? Are any groups more affected (boys, ethnic minorities, particular teaching groups)? Have we chosen the right syllabus? Right exam board? Are the teaching groups too large? Too mixed in ability? Are there textbook shortages? Does the faculty head get enough non-teaching time to monitor teaching quality? Is the faculty head too burdened with organisational jobs like arranging exchange trips? How do we appoint faculty heads? Just the same way as ordinary subject teachers? Do we probe and test management skills? Is there enough middle management training? Do pupils get enough short-term target-setting? Is course work chased up? Are we right to offer two modern languages? Or should we start the second sooner? Later? Do we look for a non-examination option in languages for the less able? There are many possible levers detectable even in these random first questions. But a head and governing body might go for one big lever: buy in a modern languages consultant to ask the questions for us!

Strategic information Few schools have yet got the right flow of strategic information for governors. We are very slowly improving the methods we use to measure school performance fairly, and governors need to be sure that what they get is more useful information – not just more information! Mainly the task is to find ways of comparing schools which take account of all their circumstances. That way we can judge how well our school compares with others in the amount it has added to what the child arrived with (this is the meaning of 'value added'). While we are waiting for this to be perfected, we can learn a great deal informally from comparisons with neighbour schools. Just examining, for instance, their main budget costs as a proportion of the total can tell us a lot. A big difference in heating costs might only indicate the age of the boiler or the architecture of the building. But a big difference in the relationship between teaching or senior management costs on the one hand and office and support staff and sophisticated information technology on the other, could be very revealing.

Shall I ever be able to manage the job?

Being a governor is a challenging and vital role. But this booklet aims to convince you that you can do it. You may feel that because you are not professionally trained and only have limited time to offer it is a task that is beyond you. The secret is to approach it at the right level, and not try to understand everything in too much detail.

- Governors are there because they are not experts. Try to feel comfortable with that idea. You represent people who may know much less than you and have even less confidence. They need someone who can see the school with their eyes but still have the courage to speak for them.
- You do not have to make any decision alone. It is the governing body which has the responsibility, not you. You also have an experienced staff who nearly all the time will run the school without a hiccup.
- You don't have to make any decision without expert advice if you need it. You may only know that something needs attention, like your car when it makes a funny noise. You need a mechanic. The 'mechanic' in a school may be a lawyer, an accountant, a builder, or an education adviser. Or a teacher. What experts may not be able to do is to spot the thing that needs looking at in the first place. They are too close and know too much to ask the idiot question The idiot question is useful. Never be afraid to ask it.
- You do not have to worry about being liable as an individual for any legal or financial trouble which the school may become involved in. The 1988 Education Act said that provided governors have acted in good faith, they will not be responsible for the consequences of action taken by the governing body, and the 1993 Act made governors even more secure by giving all schools corporate status, thus making quite clear that the risks of being sued, surcharged, fined, involve the school rather than the individual. The LEA holds insurance for schools which covers most risks, and a governing body should check for any gaps in the cover.
- Finally your perspective as an outsider is very much needed by the school. If schools can't convince you, the representatives of their users, that what they are doing works, what hope have they got with those millions outside with only their newspapers to guide them? Someone is needed to warn, to say "Hey, slow down, you move too fast." Or "They won't like that out there – needs a bit more explaining". A vital job that you can do.

Chapter 2

Governing Bodies and How They Work

Who are the governors?

The composition of governing bodies for every type of school is laid down in law: there is very little flexibility. The details are given in Appendix A. You will see that county and controlled schools and grant-maintained schools have up to five parent governors and a number of co-opted governors. In voluntary aided schools, which are usually church schools, there is only one elected parent governor and no co-opted governors (unless your school is a specialist technology or language college and has co-opted sponsor governors). A majority are foundation governors, that is governors appointed by the voluntary body which provided the school. Voluntary aided schools have one LEA governor, while grant-maintained schools have none, but there will be up to five governors appointed by the LEA in county and controlled schools.

Why these differences? Surely these are all state schools, their running costs paid from public funds, and surely the idea was that governing bodies in every school had a mixture of all the interests in the school community? Well, nearly. The differences arise from the history of the various kinds of schools, and you need to understand a little about this to make sense of their governing arrangements. Therefore a very brief account of the different kinds of schools is given in Appendix B.

Are governors' powers the same in different kinds of school? Governors powers differ very little in the various kinds of school. Grant-maintained schools are run more like an independent business, have freedom to buy and sell land and property and to borrow on the money market, and their decisions are subject to fewer external checks and appeals. Voluntary aided school governors have a few more responsibilities than in county schools. Any big differences are mentioned in this booklet as the subjects arise.

How do governing bodies work?

The first answer to this question has to be just one word – TOGETHER. It is the word which no governor should ever forget, because all the responsibilities which governors have (set out in Chapter 3) belong to the governing body acting together through decisions made at properly convened meetings with enough people present, after full discussion in which the rules laid down are observed, and by majority vote if necessary. No individual governor, not even the chairperson, can speak or act for the school unless the governors as a body so instruct him or her. The only exception is that in cases of urgency, where there is not even time to call a special meeting, the chair may take necessary action. This would be in an emergency such as a major fire, for instance.

When a governing body has made a decision, all members must abide by it and be loyal to it. This includes the head if the head has chosen to be a governor. No governor should try to continue, inside or outside the school, a battle which he or she has lost at a governors' meeting.

Information about governors' working-together rules in the conduct and organisation of their work is given in Appendix C.

The formation of a governing body

In a new school, or following changes brought in by a new Education Act, a totally new governing body is set up. After that, however, new governors join the team as and when vacancies have to be filled. Each governor has a personal period of service which is normally four years (with slight variations in voluntary aided schools). When that period expires, or the governor resigns, a replacement is appointed. In time, changes of governors will not be concentrated at the end of a particular period but will be more evenly spread; this will give more continuity.

LEA governors are appointed by the Education Committee of the local council. There is great variety in the way these governors are chosen: in some areas the political parties have a share-out in proportion to their strength on the council, in others each councillor nominates to schools in his or her ward, and, in a smaller but growing number, the LEA is not concerned at all about politics but seeks interested local people who have something to offer, even sometimes advertising publicly.

Foundation governors are appointed by the church or other voluntary body which provided the school.

Parent governors are elected by and from the parents of the school concerned by secret ballot. Election arrangements must include the opportunity to have a ballot paper sent home so parents may vote by post or, if they choose, deliver it personally to the school. A school meeting with a show of hands is not enough. Candidates may nominate themselves or be nominated by another parent. Generally they are expected to say a little bit about themselves on the form sent to parents. The 'first past the post' rule applies. The elected parent automatically becomes a governor. Parent governors may serve a full four year term if they wish even if their last child leaves the school before the four years have expired.

Teacher governors are also elected by secret ballot from and by the whole teaching staff. They have to cease to be governors when they cease to be employed at the school. In county and controlled schools there is no bar on teachers at the school or any other school becoming parent, LEA or **Co-opted governors,** but in grant-maintained schools they cannot be 'first' (ie co-opted) governors of their own school.

Co-opted governors (in grant maintained schools called 'first' governors) are chosen by the other governors from the wider community, including business, but in county and controlled schools existing co-opted governors may not vote when new ones are being elected. This restriction does not apply in grant-maintained schools.

Minor authority governors are representatives of district or parish councils where these exist in the LEA area. In such cases every LEA primary school has to have one representative of that authority.

Sponsor governors were introduced to encourage closer links between schools and business. Grant-maintained or voluntary aided schools which become technology or language colleges can appoint up to four sponsor governors. Each sponsor may put forward one or more sponsor governors, to the maximum of four sponsor governors for the school. For voluntary aided schools, a special provision guarantees that the foundation governors will always retain a majority of at least two over all other governors.

Governors' meetings, committees and business

Governors' work is carried out in meetings. The full governing body must meet at least once a term, but most nowadays meet more often than that. Occasionally a governing body will decide to have one business meeting a term and another to discuss the school less formally and concentrate on issues and policies. Some staff could helpfully attend this sort of meeting as it is a way for all to gain a better understanding of each other and of the school at work.

The governing body decides on the timing of meetings. The convenience of the majority is the objective, but there must be some give and take between governors who have other jobs and staff of the school who may live some distance away. Often the outside governors will prefer an evening, which may mean staff having to hang around after the school day. Willingness on both sides to have a mixture of times is always appreciated. Economy sometimes has to be considered, eg using the school at times when it is open and heated for other purposes.

A full governors' meeting will have an agenda circulated at least seven days before the meeting with any papers on the various items. The only exception is when a special meeting has to be called because something has come up which can't wait. In normal circumstances it is not good practice to circulate papers at the meeting itself (this is called 'tabling' papers) and governors should only accept it if an urgent matter has come up too late for details to be posted. It is inefficient to table papers because members will not have had a chance to prepare properly. It also puts some governors at a disadvantage, since not all will have the same knowledge of the background and of educational terms and procedures; some may read faster than others and, for some, English may be a second language. The nearest you can get to equality is to give all governors the time and privacy they need to read, think, and ask questions about a matter which is coming up.

The chair A chairperson is elected annually at the first meeting of the school year. The job of the chair is to lead and develop the team, to ensure that as far as possible all governors are treated alike and have an equal opportunity to contribute to the work. This means encouraging those who are lacking in confidence and curbing any who tend to dominate. The chair also has to ensure that the business is conducted efficiently with enough time allowed for the most important items, and that the meeting is conducted in accordance with the rules (see Appendix C).

The choice of chairperson should be a free and considered choice of the majority of governors. If for any reason it appears to be a foregone conclusion and governors are not really electing the person they want, the work of the governors suffers. If being 'too nice' is a problem, a sure cure is to shut your eyes and think hard about the children. If it is important to have an efficient chair whom all respect as fair, then it is a choice sometimes between offending an adult and damaging children. Put that way it is obvious what is right.

The meeting You will soon learn how meetings are managed in your particular school and this isn't a blow-by-blow account of the business side. If it is the tradition to have very formal meetings, you may like to borrow an up-to-date book on committee procedure from your library. How you, yourself, can be more effective at meetings is considered in Chapter 5. The important things to emphasise here are: (i) there must be enough people there to make decisions (this is called a quorum – see Appendix C; (ii) all governors are equal and have an equal right to contribute; (iii) it is the governing body as a whole which decides everything – not just big things like whether to appoint an additional teacher or change the length of the school day – but all the little things like which visitors to allow, whether to change the order of items on the agenda, or whether to ask someone to withdraw for part of the meeting because they stand to gain from a decision. Some of the rules set out in Appendix C are really important because they are ways of safeguarding the principles of equality of all governors, fairness of decisions, and the shared nature of governors' responsibility.

Minutes Your clerk will make a record of the meeting. Generally it will be an account of the decisions made with sometimes an indication of the main arguments on either side. It will not record every contribution or name governors unless there is a special reason. The governing body must have the business recorded as they want, however, and can even agree the wording on the spot if the matter is delicate or has to be very precisely recorded.

Since the minutes are available to anyone to read once the chair has approved them in draft, it is good practice if they are prepared as soon as possible and come to all governors at the same time, so that any governor may raise important concerns about accuracy with the chair.

Confidentiality Governors as a body decide what is to be regarded as confidential – not the head, the chair, the LEA or any individual governor. These items will be separately recorded and excluded from the published minutes or papers, since the law is that, in general, governors' business is open and their papers available to any interested party. Confidential items must be kept to a minimum. Most often they will be matters concerning a named individual – teacher, child or parent. Needless to say governors must be scrupulous to keep these items to themselves: being a governor is an office of trust and trustworthiness is essential.

Committees Governing bodies would be well advised to set up committees to deal with staff discipline and grievances and also pupil exclusions. (Grant-maintained schools are obliged to do this by law.) These matters must be kept confidential to the committee concerned since it is essential that if the individual later appeals there are enough governors who know nothing of the history of a case to hear that appeal.

Most governing bodies set up other committees or working parties: finance, premises, curriculum, and pastoral matters, for instance, to look at those matters in detail. This allows the full governing body to concentrate on general principles and have the benefit of detailed work done in advance, and it also gives more governors a chance to participate. Further information about what powers can and can't be delegated is given in Appendix C. Here it is important to note that delegating power which the governing body shares is a serious matter. The governing body should do it consciously, set out the tasks precisely and elect the members democratically. This is a decision which needs more governors present than is usually required. (See Appendix C) All governors should serve on a committee or two.

Chapter 3
What Are Governors' Responsibilities?

Someone like you can do it

Chapter 1 sets out the reasons why schools have governors and the part governors play in the general scheme of things. We now consider the detailed legal responsibilities of governors. As we go through these we shall look at the way governors carry out their tasks in practice and the kind of contribution which people without special qualifications but with a real commitment can make. Remember always that the responsibility belongs to the governing body as a whole, and in this team effort each member, while having equal status, will contribute different skills and experience.

Please do not reply that you have no skills. We are not talking about auditing accounts, writing brilliant papers, understanding legal terms, designing buildings or making a public speech. Many who have none of these talents are good listeners. Some are good at making a case and persuading others. Some are peacemakers. Some have a lot of bright ideas. Others – rare and precious people – are able to take an idea and patiently work at it. These are what one management expert calls the 'finishers', and believe me in voluntary work there aren't nearly enough of them compared with the ones who produce ideas like rabbits and then go home and watch the television till the next meeting. Maybe there are more finishers among those who don't consider themselves very clever. They may also be more likely to worry at something difficult until they've beaten it. Governing bodies need them.

Whatever your experience in life you will have learnt from it, learnt about people and their funny ways, how to manage money, how to get out of difficult corners, how to bide your time until the right moment to try an idea again, how to let people who have made a mistake or lost an argument come out with their self respect intact, how to be a good loser yourself. You won't have all these life skills but you will have some. And on a governing body they are vital.

And you will learn. How you will learn! You will never be the same again. Most people like learners, and nobody loves learners more than teachers. It seems so silly to pretend to know everything when you are in a world full of people who get great pleasure out of helping you learn.

So to work.

What do governors do?

1. Determining the character and aims of the school Governors share in setting the school's aims, and planning its future through a School Development Plan. That sounds very grand, but it isn't a professionals-only job at all. Remember you were going to tell the motor mechanic why you brought your car in? It was that new noise. You are not a builder but you tell the builder the extension is a room for granny, so you don't want it under the boys' room or on the coldest side of the house. You tell the doctor where the pain or lump is. In the shop you say the dress is for a wedding, not a conference. Right for the purpose, relevant to the problem, meeting the need. Just like a school. Someone else can tell you how many periods of social education that means, or which reading scheme.

Remember too that you are not building the school, making a garden from a virgin plot, inventing an education system. Most of it is in place, a going concern, but subject to constant adjustment. The professionals will bring all sorts of long words to the task, so don't be afraid to ask what they mean in practice. This is about a place where young people learn to be pleasant and useful adults, pick up lots of knowledge and skill, and hopefully prepare to earn a living, bring up a family and be good members of society. Maybe the head will bring you a draft or show you an earlier version of the Development Plan. Nothing wrong with that – you have to start somewhere. But try to move to an acceptance that your contribution is best at the brainstorming stage. It's easier for ordinary people to say something useful about a paper if they have talked about its purpose and contributed some ideas.

As far as the Development Plan is concerned, this is a statement of priorities for a few years ahead such as I expect you have, in your head at least, for your home or in your job. Just like these activities, the Development Plan will be closely related to money – unrealistic otherwise. So the Plan will link up with the budget. It should have targets for each stage, and it should say how you are going to judge whether you have met them:
- Better behaviour? What does that mean? Fewer exclusions, fewer in detention, more gold stars?
- More fluent readers? How many, by how much?

- Expansion of out-of-school activities? More clubs, more teachers running clubs, more children joining clubs? Or more low achieving 14-year-old boys in clubs?

2. The budget Each school now has its own budget and the governors in a broad sense look after it: this is part of Local Management of Schools (LMS). The budget covers almost everything – staff salaries, books and equipment, routine maintenance of the building, water, electricity, telephone charges, exam fees and various services brought from the LEA and elsewhere. Governors consider the needs of the school as advised by the head and staff, discuss priorities, and each year agree a budget setting out how available funds should be spent. They must give the staff reasonable freedom within particular headings to meet needs as they arise. Any under or overspend can be carried over, but governors must not deliberately plan to overspend, and too large a surplus also sometimes raises difficult questions. The ideal is just a modest contingency allowance to meet the unexpected, though obviously any long term plans may require setting money aside for this each year.

You will almost certainly have a finance committee. In deciding whom to vote onto it, don't be mesmerised by dark suits. It's excellent if you have an expert to help a little, as long as you know that means helping others to do it, not doing it for them. All governors share the responsibility for spending and it is dangerous if they don't spread the responsibility so that all interest groups are represented, including a parent and a teacher. Don't make the mistake of getting into the tens and units level of checking: you are not book-keepers. Stick to the figures with three or four noughts. Don't forget that money is not a mystery with a life of its own, but the wherewithal to buy the necessities of learning.

3. Staffing In agreement with head and senior staff the governors agree the staffing needs of the school. Most governors will wish to spend as much as they can afford on teachers. Local management has shown, however, that the balance between teaching and support staff and between staff on the one hand and facilities and equipment on the other do repay discussion if the money is to be used more effectively. The aim is to support the teaching process as much as you can and free the teachers to do what they are trained for.

Head and deputy are selected by the governors after public advertisement. The governing body elects a panel to do the selection process, again with a good mix of governors. (The whole governing body must approve the choice at the end.) This means the group draws up the advertisement, the job description, the person specification and the short-list. The LEA will help in LEA schools. The same group should be involved throughout.

Take it seriously – it is the most important thing you ever do. But don't be paralysed with fear. In LEA schools you will get advice from their experts about what qualifications and experience to look for, and what kind of interviewing process to set up, whether or not to have practical exercises, etc. They may even lay on a training session in your school for those involved. They have a right to send a representative to advise you at any stage, but the panel makes the choice. In a grant-maintained school, you may be able to buy in advice. Remember, because this is reassuring, that if you've had reasonably good applications any of those short-listed should, in professional terms, be able to do the job, so you will be looking for that something special – often the understanding the person has of your sort of school. Listen more carefully than you have ever done in your life.

Governors are also entitled to play a part in choosing teachers. They decide themselves how much direct involvement they want in this process, but they remain responsible. It is therefore wise to ensure some governor participation in selection panels, ideally on some kind of rota. Look at the kind of governor duty systems suggested in Chapter 5 which may suggest a basis for rotas. Heads are often quite happy to let governors delegate teacher appointments to them, but the wise ones value the fresh perspective, the support for their choice and the commitment all have to someone they helped choose.

In all selection processes remember equal opportunities principles. This simply means showing no prejudice against any candidate, or putting any at a disadvantage, whatever their background. You will mostly hear of this in the context of the law on racial and sex discrimination I'm sure, but think of other forms as well. Ensure that you set aside any prejudice unrelated to the job (eg against gaudy socks or certain kinds of accent); give equal time to each, listen as carefully to the last as the first (easy to say but the process is very tiring); ensure that for the most part you ask the same questions of all, and even that you watch, as the sun comes round, that it isn't in the candidate's eyes. Constantly check and recheck against the criteria you have agreed upon, make notes and hold on to them. Both these bits of guidance will not only help you to be fair and rational, but you may need to justify your preference if there is a complaint.

4. The curriculum The governing body has to ensure that the national curriculum is taught, that religious education and worship are provided, and that any children with special needs get the help they require. In secondary schools governors must ensure that all pupils have a programme of sex education which includes information about HIV and AIDS. In primary schools, governors have the choice of whether to provide sex education beyond that included in the National Curriculum.

Governors help decide what other subjects are taught in the school but are not responsible for *how* subjects are taught. That is a professional's job.

Governors' responsibilities for children with special educational needs are highlighted in the law. Over and above their general responsibility for the curriculum, they must satisfy themselves at all times that the school identifies and makes proper provision for such children. There is a government Code of Practice which must be observed. Governors are recommended – but not obliged – to designate one governor to take special interest in this area of the work.

Most governing bodies establish a curriculum working party. It cannot be a committee with delegated powers because legally curriculum responsibility must remain with the whole governing body, though of course a small group may collect material, set out alternative courses of action and make recommendations.

A good curriculum working party will be familiarising itself with the curriculum on a rolling programme, going through each part of the school's work in turn and asking the member of staff responsible to come to the committee and tell them about it. Apart from building up knowledge, it makes it easier to look critically at a whole subject area if it is causing concern.

Apart from their legal tasks, governors are responsible for the school's effectiveness and should be fully aware of the various ways in which its success can be measured. They should be satisfied that children achieve the very best they are capable of and that the school is continually seeking to improve every aspect of its work. Governors are at their least confident in approaching curriculum matters, partly because it is here that they feel their lack of professional expertise matters most, and partly because they know professionals are touchy about this 'holy of holies' or secret garden as it is often called. There is no need for them to feel inadequate. Ever since there were schools there has been acceptance that, while teachers are experts in the 'how' of education and must be left to get on with it, deciding what is taught – curriculum content – is a matter for democratic bodies representing the public. At different times and in different proportions the responsibility has been channelled through local authorities (mainly so between 1870 and 1988) and central government (since 1988 through the National Curriculum) but always with governors key players at school level. Even if they know nothing about reading schemes they can, with help, compare the outcomes of one method with another. They soon recognise a child who is reading with understanding and pleasure and they don't need to be told that reading is the foundation of most learning. Please read again at this point what is said in Chapter 1 (page 6) about the meaning of 'strategic' in describing the level at which governors work and the ways in which governors can play a part in school improvement.

5. Personnel matters Governors are in effect the personnel officers for the school. They establish policies on staff discipline and grievance procedures. They usually have a committee to deal with these matters to ensure that there are always other governors available who have no knowledge of what went before to constitute an appeal committee if necessary. They settle the pay of the head and deputy following an annual review. Criteria for this are set out in government guidelines. They may make extra pay allowances to teachers in circumstances which are also clearly laid down. In voluntary aided (mostly church) schools and grant-maintained schools the governors are actually the employers of the staff, but in county and controlled schools, although the governors have most of the functions of an employer, the staff member's actual contract is with the LEA.

6. Pupils and discipline The governors share the responsibility for good behaviour with the head who takes measures in the context of any principles that the governing body has set down. Governors have a key role in promoting good behaviour and would be well advised to have a written policy which they monitor regularly. Guidelines on issues like bullying, for instance, give staff confidence that they are acting fairly and consistently when they respond to pupil misbehaviour and also help governors if they have to intervene in an exclusion or as a result of a parental complaint. Only the head may exclude a pupil and when this happens the parents may appeal to governors if they wish. The governors may require the pupil to be reinstated if they are not convinced that the decision was correct.

7. Premises Governors see that the building is kept in good order and that it is safe and healthy. They will probably have a committee to do this. General care and maintenance come out of the school budget. Capital projects have to be approved by the LEA which in turn must get permission from the government to put them in a building programme.

8. Communication It is here that governors have one of their most important responsibilities. Because they are accountable for how well they have looked after the school, and because they must ensure that the school is responsive to those who use it, their role as a communicating link is vital. They are the school's ambassadors outside its gates and the people who can best convey parent and community concerns to the school, smooth the path to the school for those who find it hard to approach schools, and generally rub down any sharp corners and fill any cracks in the school's own communications system. It is also a delicate area, since professionals often see communication as part of authority and fear that it will get out of their control. Governors must, therefore, be careful to ensure that as a body they sing the same tune, keep in close touch with the head, and are accurate and discreet in everything they say.

9. Parents Governors also have specific responsibilities, namely to see that parents get all the information to which they are entitled by law, through the school prospectus and in other ways. (You will find a list of information requirements in your *DfEE Guide to the Law*.) Governors also need to ensure that parents are fully aware of their right to see governors' papers and various school policies and schemes of work as well as their children's own records, and of their rights in respect of a child with special needs. Finally, governors have to publish an annual report on their work for distribution to all parents, and arrange a meeting at which parents can discuss governors' work and any aspect of the running of the school. This report and meeting should not be regarded as just an annual chore. It will inevitably take some time for parents to realise the accountability of governors and their scope for influencing them, but keep at it. You should read a *Do-it-Better Guide* on annual reports and meetings published by *Action for Governors Information and Training (AGIT)* if your governing body is keen to improve (address on page 44).

10. Pupil admissions Every school has a standard admission number based on its past intake combined with its space. Places must be offered up to this number each year, but governors may ask for an increase or a reduction if they think it necessary. (Ask your LEA about this.) Every school is also bound by criteria for giving places if the school is over-subscribed. In a county or controlled school these are drawn up by the LEA after consultation with governors, and they are administered by the LEA, ie the authority decides who gets places. In aided and grant-maintained schools the governors establish the rules or criteria, which must be published, and they also decide who should be admitted in the light of those rules. Church schools may give preference to church-goers. Otherwise admission rules generally centre around proximity or attendance at recognised feeder schools; having brothers or sisters at the school; medical needs; and, in some cases, special ability or aptitude. If they are unsuccessful in gaining a place for their child, parents have the right to appeal to an independent appeals panel, set up by the LEA or the governing body. Where governing bodies are responsible – in the case of aided and grant-maintained schools – they must ensure that governor members appointed to the panel have taken no part in earlier admissions decisions if parents are to have confidence in their independence.

11. Inspection All schools are inspected at regular intervals.

National inspection programmes are organised by the Office for Standards in Education (OFSTED). The governors normally meet the inspectors before they begin and have a chance to talk about the school; the governing body also has to arrange a meeting for parents to meet the inspectors without teachers or governors present (unless they happen to be parents of the school). After the inspection, the inspecting team meets the governors to tell them its findings. It is the governing body which is responsible for drawing up an action plan to respond to the findings of the report, and for checking regularly and reporting to parents on the progress of this plan.

How to Be a Good Representative

In Chapter 1 we talked about how governing bodies have developed in history and about one role they have always had: to represent the public interest in schools. In this wider sense your job is always to represent others and to bear in mind especially the needs of the families who use your school and the community they live in. Representing others in something as vital as their children's schooling is an awesome task, and you are right to take it seriously. But throughout this book you are reminded that it is a job for an ordinary person who is interested and committed, that you don't have to do it on your own, that you can always get expert advice, and that you can learn to be effective.

Understanding the needs of your community

If you live in an area where two thirds of the adult population has university degrees your task will not be quite the same as that of the governor in an area where two thirds are unemployed, and the pressures on you will be different.

In the first case you may have to restrain parents who think all their children are gifted, whose interest in special needs is that slow learners must not hold others back, and who want the curriculum in primary schools geared to entry to private schools and that of the secondary school to classics, separate sciences and Oxbridge! In the second, you may have to work hard to ensure that your school has high enough expectations of all children and that their parents appreciate that their support is crucial to their children's success. You may also have to try to make the school less judgmental about families who can't cope with their everyday problems and for whom ensuring their children's attendance at school, suitably dressed and fed, seems an unattainable goal, never mind hearing them read. But in both cases you will be concerned that *all* children are given a chance to do as well as they can, that parents understand the aims of the school for all its different pupils, and that the school communicates effectively with parents of all classes both about their own children's progress and problems and its policies and needs. Most schools take communication very seriously these days, but many still communicate in language which is not accessible to everybody and some, with all the kindness and compassion in the world, do thus make parents feel inadequate. You have a big job in such an area which will call for all your tact and persistence.

The community isn't just made up of parents, and you will also want to ensure as a thoughtful representative that the school is a good neighbour. Does your school think about the community's reaction to everything it does, about the neighbourhood's under-used resources and its possible need (and right) to use the school's resources? It's so easy to see neighbours only as a source of complaints about behaviour on the buses and cans and sweet wrappers in front gardens. It is always worthwhile for instance to invite the local residents' association to come in to see the first plans of an extension, including the landscaping planned, before the builders arrive. Near neighbours will appreciate being warned by leaflet of the date of the school concert and being asked to be tolerant about parking. They will especially welcome being invited to come to the last rehearsal.

Perhaps you as a governor will be the person who gently reminds the school that lots of people in the community have skills, especially the older ones, which they could share with children. And perhaps you will be the one who spots groups within the community who could benefit by sharing some resources the school can offer.

You don't, of course, have to side automatically with the public just because you represent them. Listening, and doing your bit to make the school listen, doesn't take away your freedom to make up your mind when interests conflict, and no governor is a delegate from any group. Nevertheless all governors should take the representing part of the job seriously, not just in general but on behalf of their particular interest.

LEA representatives will be the ones who sometimes have to look beyond the narrower interests of one school to the needs of the local community. Foundation governors will see the school also as part of the church family, demonstrating a particular set of values through education. Co-opted governors will be especially concerned with the wider community, and all that has been said about the school being a good neighbour applies to them particularly.

But it is the elected governors, those who represent parents or teachers, who have the most weighty problems of representation, since they have been chosen by their fellows and represent a distinctive interest group.

Representing parents

If you are an elected parent governor you will feel particularly keenly the responsibility of representing others, firstly because parents are, by any standard, the most concerned group and the most in need of a link with the school; secondly because they trusted you to do it; and thirdly, because you soon realise that it's by no means as easy as you thought.

You may even have been told that it's not your job to speak for parents, that you just bring a typical individual parent's point of view to the discussion. This may be a genuine misunderstanding of the situation on the part of whoever said it, or a deliberate attempt to restrict your role, but either way it's wrong. Of course you represent those who elected you. You are not a delegate - that's a different matter. Sometimes, when people serve on committees or go to a conference, they go there with clear instructions to vote in a certain way. Those they represent will go through every item and say: support that, oppose this, abstain on the other. This is not a governor's role. A governor listens to the views of others, reads as much about the subject as possible, and in the end does what he or she thinks best for the children in the school.

So what does being a representative entail? First, it means listening all you can. Second, it means conveying the concerns of your group to the governing body and thirdly, it means reporting back matters of interest.

Then, at the meeting, some schools will have a regular place on the agenda for parent governors' reports. In others you may be unable to get a hearing or told it isn't the time or place. As for reporting back, a few governors will be told everything is confidential, which is just plain wrong. Others may be given a bit of space in the head's newsletter for a regular report. If you are one of the unlucky ones, don't simply compare yourself with the most lucky. We all have to start from where we are and see how much we can move forward. Having some good practice to refer to always helps.

The wrong way to do it A parent governor who finds any possible or impossible space in a governors' meeting to bring up without warning every bit of school gate tittle tattle, far-fetched misunderstanding of school policy or individual complaint, is a menace. Generally, it's done in innocence or in desperation because nobody will tell you how else to do it. A governor who gossips about teachers' off-record remarks or the private affairs of children or families gleaned from visits to the school is a disgrace. So is one who reports what went on at a meeting in full technicolour, how everybody voted, who made the head look silly, who took Councillor Bighead down a peg or two, who lost her temper, who mispronounced all the long words. Being a governor is 'an office of trust under the Crown' and that means professional standards in a privileged position.

Good communication The governing body is the place for general concerns. There are other ways of dealing with individual problems (see below). If you have changes in the reading scheme or curriculum options on the agenda, or an alteration in school rules or organisation, you need to listen wherever you can to get a feeling for parents' reactions and bring them up at the right moment. Whether or not you agree with them you should report them conscientiously. A very good practice is to ensure that parents' meetings or events are attended by as many governors as possible: this is the best place to pick up concerns. If many parents are agitated about something which isn't on the agenda you must try to get it there.

Reporting back is a matter of using whatever means is acceptable to the school. Don't be put off by suggestions that it isn't your job or that you should wait for the minutes. But be certain you are accurate, be scrupulous about anything classified as confidential, and confine yourself to decisions and, if appropriate, the reasons for them. Don't reveal how people voted or what they said, and don't repeat any spicy bits. You must protect the unity of the governing body and never put colleagues in a bad light.

Individual concerns Some heads actually discourage governors from listening to parents' individual concerns and advise directing them straight to the school. This is unrealistic. It is natural for parents, who might fear that their worry is too trivial to bother teachers, to try it on a friendly governor in the supermarket first. Anyway you can often correct misunderstandings from your own knowledge and you can certainly reassure parents that their concern isn't trivial and that the teacher or head will want to hear it. Encourage them to go to the school, go with them if it helps, or in an extreme case take the matter up for them. But never try to solve it yourself and never by-pass the head. Your job is to smooth the path to the school in every way you can, and thus try to stop small troubles becoming big ones.

Full governors in every sense When parent governors were a novelty, they often suffered from being treated as something less than full governors, as though they were just there to give a parent's point of view and not to share fully in the work of the governing body. We hope that this is a thing of the past, but parent governors do sometimes have to be watchful that they are included in everything. It might be suggested, perhaps, that they should keep out of a discussion on changes which affect their child's class or teacher, or that they are not reliable on confidential matters - an insulting suggestion which should never be allowed to pass. Parent governors like others should not take part in anything from which they might profit (eg if they did catering for parties and the school wanted to get quotes for a function) or where their own child was being discussed (eg in an exclusion).

Representing teachers

Most of what has been said above about parent governors applies equally to teachers. You too have an important task to bring teachers' general concerns to the governing body and ensure that they are taken account of in making decisions, even in a case where you yourself cannot agree. For like a parent governor, you are a representative not a delegate. You should ensure that the agenda and papers are always available in the staffroom before meetings so that other members of staff can comment on anything which is coming up, and that minutes are similarly available as soon as they have been approved in draft by the chair. You do not need to wait until the whole governing body has ratified them. Like parent governors, you should only relate decisions when reporting back: no names, no spicy bits, and you should be scrupulously silent about any confidential items.

Teacher governors have a wider representational role in that they are able through the governing body to ensure that decisions about teachers are made in a fair and open way and that staff interests are always taken account of in decisions that concern them directly. They can ensure that the governing body is well informed in its discussions on the curriculum and build a better understanding between teachers and governors. It is important that they should not be barred from serving on any committee or selection panel just because it comes close to their professional concerns: they are eligible to help select senior staff, to take part in a disciplinary enquiry concerning a colleague or serve on a pay committee. The only restriction is that which applies to all governors, namely that they should keep out of any decision from which they stand to gain personally - 'more than the generality of teachers'. You may not, of course, *wish* to be involved in some matter which affects a close friend: it is your right to refuse. But no-one else should wrongly exclude you.

Teacher representatives will often feel inhibited in speaking freely in a meeting lest they upset the head by taking a different line, knowing well that the consequences for their career could be serious. It is a great pity that the potential contribution of teacher governors should be lost in this way, and hopefully, as the system matures, heads will feel able to reassure teacher representatives that their confident participation and their advocacy of staff interests will be welcomed and never punished in any way. Schools will certainly be the richer for it.

Being an Effective Member of a Team

Since it is the governing body, not the individual, which has the responsibility, its effectiveness depends on how well its members work as a team. However clever or well-informed they are, they will not be effective school governors unless they are good team players. Indeed, you can only be described as effective in terms of your contribution to the team.

What is a good team?

A good team has a common purpose, whether it is to beat the next village at cricket or raise money for famine relief. Everybody understands the purpose and sometimes they remind each other of it. The members respect each other as equals. They attach importance to developing their skills through training and experience. They look after weaker members. They co-ordinate their efforts and pull together. They are loyal to each other but they also have high expectations of each other and keep each other up to the mark. They all know the rules and keep them. They accept responsibility for their own work, and know that if things go wrong they share the blame. They don't find scapegoats. They know they have to work with the colleagues they have so they don't look to solve problems by getting rid of people.

Does all that apply to the governing body? It certainly does, especially the last bit. In nearly all forms of voluntary work you have to work with those who volunteer. You may be able to influence people and you may be able to reduce the damage less suitable people can do, but in the end, you will probably have to find ways of working with them. It is all but impossible to remove a governor who doesn't want to be removed. Perhaps that's a good thing: it might not be healthy if groups could too easily exclude the difficult members. What teams can do - and this is probably the most important statement in the book - is to build the qualities they value into a culture so strong that it changes people, absorbs them into itself, and now and then persuades the odd individual who can't live up to those values to call it a day.

Good teamwork for governors

The common purpose You don't need anyone to tell you what your common purpose is. It is to serve and support and guide that school to the very best of your ability, and ensure that it provides the finest possible education for every child. That means that you want it to aim with your help for the highest standards, to be always self-critical and self-improving, to be humane and tolerant, to value children in all their diversity, to use its resources well, to appreciate and develop its staff and treat them fairly, to provide a safe and pleasant environment for learning, to encourage and involve parents and listen to their concerns, and to be a good neighbour.

Do you as a governing body spell that out often enough? Sometimes people can become so obsessed with being organised, scoring points, being right, being clever, getting their own back, balancing the books, winning an argument or patching up a problem, that they lurch through those long agendas like a joy rider without maps or brakes. It is helpful sometimes to stop and remind each other what it is all for. Make enough space in your meetings from time to time to review your priorities and principles.

Training and development Every governor can improve performance by reading, talking to experts, taking up training and getting involved in the school. Training should always be on the agenda, literally. Those who don't ever go to training sessions should be made to feel uncomfortable - part of your high expectations of each other must be a bit of public shame. A governing body can plan its total involvement in training so that somehow most subjects get covered and shared. If your LEA offers a school-based session on working together, go for it: team training is in many ways the best.

You can't be a good governor unless you spend some time in the school when it is working, not going on lightning tours of classrooms but getting absorbed into lessons and seeing how children learn. This is another activity which should be expected of everybody, with slackers given a hard time. Governors as individuals have no automatic right to visit the school and obviously you should ask if it's convenient and be as courteous as you would in anyone else's place of work. You go either because the head invites you or because the governors have so decided. The best thing is if the governing body agrees on a system of individual attachment to the school: a governor adopting a class and going up with the class, so seeing the whole learning programme and getting to know one group of children very well, is ideal in a primary school. Attachment to a subject or activity is good in any kind of school, but best of all, perhaps, is a month of duty for each governor during which he or she is the first point of contact with the school for anything it needs, from giving out swimming badges to helping appoint a teacher. Some time during the month you promise to go in and observe children at work, as well as responding as often as you can to requests.

Needless to say you will not in any way intervene in the lesson and certainly make it clear that the object is to learn, not judge. Share the teacher's enthusiasm - there is no better way of building a lasting good relationship. Teacher governors are often the best people to fix up suitable pairings: make sure the teacher you visit is keen too. There is no point at all in forcing yourself on a terrified teacher: build on positives and let the confidence grow.

Supporting timid colleagues Do your bit to bring shy governors into the discussion and protect any who are being badly treated or unreasonably excluded from tasks. Make sure that your governing body plans and properly manages the business of induction of new recruits: sometimes this is painfully mishandled.

Familiarity with rules Ensure that you know the rules of working together (see Appendix C). People who abuse power often take advantage if others aren't sure how things ought to be done. Don't compromise about observing the rules. They ensure open and democratic working and the rights of all governors to take part. Be wary of cosy habits: 'in' jokes, informal ways of working, easy assumptions that everybody agrees when some governors may be frightened to disagree unless asked. Too much informality is worse than the reverse when it comes to excluding people, and it isn't bureaucratic to ask politely for things to be done properly. A and B teams easily develop from too much chumminess.

Accepting responsibility You would be amazed how often governors, when talking to others, refer to the governing body as 'they'.

© ACE 1996 Published by the ADVISORY CENTRE FOR EDUCATION ● 33

It's a real give-away, and implies a wish to be detached from the follies and cruelties occasionally found in all groups. When you *think* 'WE' you are progressing. If bad things happen, all of you sat there and let them happen, even if some did nothing. The silent ones were either too slow finding their place, not familiar enough with the rules, or too nice. The cure for being too nice is to think hard about the children. Better upset an adult than hurt them. Accepting responsibility means planning the work. If you feel you are always consulted after the event, ask the head to finish off his or her report by telling you what's coming up before you meet next: then you can plan. There is no participation in the past. Loyalty to decisions made together is also the hallmark of a good team: you may lose the argument on a matter very important to you, but you must still support majority decisions and be loyal to colleagues.

At the meeting

After a good meeting everybody goes home feeling that the business has been efficiently dealt with, that wise decisions have been made and that each one has had a say. You as an effective governor can play your part in achieving that.

Preparation You will of course read all the papers carefully beforehand and ask an appropriate person - perhaps the LEA's governor trainer or a colleague - if there is a point you don't understand. Try to form some kind of opinion: you may change it as you listen to others, but it is irritating to colleagues if a governor just uses time thinking aloud.

Contributing Don't feel you have to say something on every item or ask questions just to show you are awake. When you do want to contribute, be brief and to the point. Don't be anecdotal: unless how Mandy felt about the new maths scheme or what Mrs Brown said about the dinners really adds something, keep it to yourself.

Tactics If you have a very strong view about a matter, it may pay not to show your hand too quickly. Argue around it a while and put your points as though they were questions. Grant that there may be other ways of looking at it. Praise good points when others make them. Hard to say why, but people often suspect anyone with strong convictions and a light in their eye, and might be influenced to turn the other way. It's not very rational or very nice, but many a good case has been lost through enthusiasm displayed too soon.

Behaviour Be courteous to everyone. Don't be afraid to say if you don't understand something. You are unlikely to be the only one. Anyway some people enjoy feeling better informed and most love explaining things. Ask for more information to be produced when you need to but always be sure you know what you are going to do with it when you get it. If you are so nervous that something you say comes out all wrong and sounds aggressive be quick to admit it and say you didn't mean quite that. Indeed always be quick to say sorry. Pride is a useless thing to have in a team. Don't be upset if you had an idea which got ridiculed some time ago and now they've acted upon it in the school without a word of acknowledgement. It's more important that the right thing is done for the children than that someone gets the credit: you may not be able to have both. Don't bring up any old thing under 'Any Other Business' because you don't know how else to get it discussed. AOB, if you have it at all, is for strictly unforeseen and really urgent matters, and then only with the chair's permission. Better to ask at the beginning for an addition to the agenda if it's substantial and urgent. If it's not urgent, ask for it to be included next time.

Round and about

Needless to say, you will be a willing governor and try to do your share of the chores. You should be on at least one committee, probably two. You will go to as many school events as you can. Your commitment and your willingness to learn will soon make friends in the school, especially if you always share teachers' enthusiasms, take an interest in their special contributions - a curriculum innovation, out-of-school activity or extra qualification. Relationships with teachers are so important. Often they have strange ideas about governors based on lack of contact and may even be fearful. Try to think of ways in which they and the governing body can work together and get to know each other. Show concern about their working conditions and amenities. Always speak up for fair and open decision-making on matters that concern teachers, and do your share to protect teacher governors from being excluded from governors' duties just because they are teachers. In other words do everything you can to establish their equal status and important role.

Governors as ambassadors

You will always remember what is said in Chapter 4 about being scrupulously careful to keep your counsel on confidential matters and reporting governors' discussions discreetly and professionally. You will also be aware that the head is the school's paid public relations officer, among other duties, and you will not take upon yourself the sole responsibility of selling the school to the community.

Nevertheless a well-informed and committed governor can be a most important ambassador and people will take a lot of notice of what such a person says about the school - to which you will, of course, always be loyal in public, even at times when you may be struggling with some problem or disagreement. If you spend time in classes you will be able to reassure parents that schools aren't the madhouses sometimes portrayed in the press, where teachers pursue extreme theories and chaos reigns. You will be able to convince them that the great majority of teachers are dedicated, moderate and in control of the learning process. You will be able to make the connections for parents between classroom activity and the learning goals to which it is directed. This sort of ambassador, someone who really knows the school and is part of the community, is worth more than thousands of pounds spent on marketing.

The headteacher

You will soon discover that relations with the headteacher are what make being a governor wonderful - or very hard. When the relationship is good, open, friendly, sharing and trusting, it makes the job easy and pleasant. If there are difficulties, do make some allowances. Firstly, remember what a frighteningly responsible and exposed job he or she has. It can be hard for heads to share those awesome responsibilities without being fearful lest some incompetent amateur or loose cannon lands them in trouble. *You* know you are full of good motives and commitment, with no desire to run the school, but the head may take some time to be reassured. Remember too that many heads, especially those whose memories go back to the days when political party games were not unknown on governing bodies, have had bad experiences of governors, and even today many governors *do* behave in an inappropriate and threatening way.

Just go on being interested and courteous and show respect for the head's knowledge and experience. Demonstrate that you will do practical and controversial things for the school, as well as engaging in policy discussions. Don't compromise on your right to be informed and involved, but don't forget, in your eagerness to make suggestions, to praise when praise is appropriate and show your attachment and commitment to the school. Some day you will have a chance to support the head and the school through a testing time or a really sticky patch, and after that everything will change. It is changing anyway, all the time, with your help.

Appendix A

Composition of governing bodies of county, controlled, and maintained special schools

Under 100 pupils:
2 parent governors
2 LEA governors
1 teacher governor
Headteacher (if he or she wishes)
either 2 foundation + 1 co-opted (controlled schools)
or 3 co-opted (county and special schools)

100 – 299 pupils:
3 parent governors
3 LEA governors
1 teacher governor
Headteacher (if he or she wishes)
either 3 foundation + 1 co-opted (controlled)
or 4 co-opted (county and special schools)

300 – 599 pupils:
4 parent governors
4 LEA governors
2 teacher governors
Headteacher (if he or she wishes)
either 4 foundation + 1 co-opted (controlled schools)
or 5 co-opted (county and special schools)

600 pupils or more:
5 parent governors
5 LEA governors
2 teacher governors
Headteacher (if he or she wishes)
either 4 foundation + 2 co-opted (controlled schools)
or 6 co-opted (county and special schools)

LEAs have the option to drop the largest category of 600 pupils or more and treat such schools the same as those of 300 – 599, thus establishing 16 as the largest size of governing body. This is the only flexibility allowed on numbers. In making co-options, governors must bear in mind the need for representation from the business community. One representative governor must be appointed in place of a co-opted governor in certain circumstances set out in Section 7, Education (No 2) Act 1986.

All LEA primary schools must have a representative of any minor authority, i.e. district or parish council, replacing one LEA nominee.

Composition of governing bodies of aided and special agreement schools

Regardless of size:
At least 1 LEA governor
In primary schools, at least 1 representative of the minor authority, if any
At least 1 parent governor
At least 1 teacher governor in schools of under 300
At least 2 teacher governors in schools of 300 and over
Headteacher (if he or she wishes)
Foundation governors – who must outnumber other governors (including the headteacher even if he or she has chosen not to be a governor) as follows –
by 2 in governing bodies with up to 18 members and by 3 if the total number of governors is 19 or more. One foundation governor must always be, at the time of appointment, a parent of a pupil.

Composition of governing body of grant-maintained schools

5 parent governors in secondary schools
3 - 5 parent governors in primary schools
Headteacher as ex officio member (s/he does not have the option to decline to be a governor)
1 or 2 teacher governors
First or foundation governors who must outnumber other governors. Sponsor governors do not count as "other governors" for this purpose.
In former county schools, at least two first governors must be parents of the school, and at least two must be members of the local community. First governors must also include members of the local business community. One person may satisfy two or more of these requirements.

Appendix B

Different Kinds of Schools and their Governing Bodies

County schools These are schools provided originally by the LEA, which owns the buildings and pays all the maintenance costs. The LEA therefore has a substantial share on the governing body, varying with the size of the school. The LEA in consultation with governors draws up the admission criteria and decides which children get places. The LEA is the employer of the teachers. Religious education is given but it is non-denominational and while being basically Christian it also reflects the beliefs of other faiths established in the area.

Controlled schools These are schools originally provided by a voluntary body but unable at the time of the 1944 Education Act to afford building maintenance. They are run exactly like county schools except that there is some representation of the voluntary body among the governors and they may give religious education in accordance with their faith if parents ask for it.

Voluntary aided schools These are part of the state system and their teachers and all their running costs are paid by the LEA. The voluntary body owns the building, however, and has to pay for outside repairs and maintenance. In return it has a majority on the governing body and there is correspondingly less representation of parents as such and no co-options. The governors draw up the admissions criteria and decide which individual children get places. They are the employers of the staff. Religious education and worship are in accordance with the trust deed of the school which generally means that it is Church of England, Roman Catholic or other religion, since in most cases the voluntary body is a church.

Grant-maintained schools These are schools which under the 1988 Education Act decided to opt out of LEA control and receive their funds directly through the Secretary of State, though the money still comes out of the LEA budget. Thus they have no LEA governors, and co-opted or 'first' governors are in a majority. Where the school was formerly voluntary aided the first governors represent the foundation. Former county schools co-opt them from the wider community. The governors are the employers of their staff and they have control of admissions and must publish their criteria. Like all other kinds of school in the public system they have to offer the National Curriculum, and they must comply with most of the requirements applying to other such schools but their decisions are subject to less external appeals.

Appendix C

Rules and Good Practices for Working Together

1. **Corporate responsibility** All the responsibilities belong to the governing body working together. An individual governor has no authority, except the chair in certain special circumstances.
2. **Meetings** Governors meet at least once a term. Notice of meetings must be given, with the agenda, at least seven days in advance. Where urgent matters arise which cannot await the next meeting the chair may call a special meeting at shorter notice. Any three governors may also request a special meeting and this request must be granted.
3. **Chair and vice-chair** Governors elect a chair and vice-chair annually, in the first meeting of the school year. No employee of the school is eligible.
4. **Non-attendance** Governors who, without permission, fail to attend meetings for six months automatically cease to be members.
5. **The headteacher** The head may be a full voting governor but has the option to decline membership by giving written notice. All headteachers, whether governors or not, have the right to attend meetings of the governing body and its committees (but see 14 below).
6. **Chair's power in emergency** The chair may act on behalf of the governing body in urgent matters where there is no time even to call a special meeting. He or she must report that action to the governing body.
7. **Voting** Governors make decisions by majority vote. There is only one matter on which a secret ballot of the governing body is required by law: when considering whether to ballot for GM status; otherwise governors themselves decide whether on any matter a secret ballot is desirable.
8. **Quorum** For a governing body to be able to make decisions, one third of the total membership, the latter calculated to include any vacancies, must be present. For certain decisions a higher quorum of two thirds of governors in post and eligible to vote is required (note the different basis of calculation). The most important are when any new governors are being selected (eg co-options) or when power is being delegated to committees. (See *Guide to the Law*)
9. **Committees** Governors are well advised to set up committees of at least three members each to deal with staff discipline and pupil exclusions respectively, and must ensure that there are enough governors remaining without knowledge of the matter in question to serve on an appeal panel if necessary. This is a legal requirement in the case of grant-maintained schools which must

Appendix C

also set up an admissions committee of at least three governors, one being the head. Appeals panels must have at least as many members as the committee making the original decision. (There is a concession on this - intended especially for small schools - whereby the requirement on numbers is waived if fewer than six governors are eligible to serve.) Otherwise governors set up such committees as they need although grant-maintained schools are required to set up certain committees where necessary (see the DfEE's GM *A Guide to the Law*).

10. Delegation Some other functions may be delegated to a committee if governors wish. There are many exceptions which are given in full in your Guide to the Law. Among those which cannot be delegated are religious education and worship, curriculum decisions, whether to go to ballot on GM status, admissions, selecting new governors, the annual report to parents, appointing a new head or deputy (though a panel may choose and recommend) and changes in the character of the school.

11. Chairing committees In general governors may elect chairs when they set up committees or leave the committee to choose its own. In LEA schools no employee of the school may chair a committee with delegated power. This is not so in grant-maintained schools.

12. Rescinding a decision If a governing body rescinds a decision they have previously made, the item must have been on the agenda circulated.

13. Co-options In county and controlled schools co-opted members may not vote in new co-options. This does not apply in grant-maintained schools.

14. Declaring an interest A governor may play no part in a discussion, or vote, if he or she or a spouse or close relative stands to gain any advantage from the outcome: that governor may also be asked to withdraw if governors so decide. In the case of teachers this is defined as an interest 'greater than the generality of teachers in the school'. The head may not be present when governors make a decision whether to reinstate an excluded pupil. He or she and others with a direct interest may be given a separate opportunity to state their case.

15. Visitors to meetings The governing body decides which, if any, visitors it invites to its meetings, either on a regular basis or for a particular occasion.

16. Minutes and papers The governing body's agenda and related papers, and their minutes once they have been approved in draft by the chair, may be seen on request by any member of the public as well as staff and parents. Excluded items will be those which the governing body itself has classified as confidential to protect individual privacy.

Useful Organisations

Government departments and organisations

Department for Education and Employment (DfEE)
Sanctuary Buildings
Great Smith Street
London SW1P 3BT
(0171 925 5000)

Welsh Office
Education Department
Government Buildings
Cathays Park
Cardiff CF1 3NQ (01222 823207)

Office For Standards In Education (OFSTED)
Alexandra House
33 Kingsway, London WC2B 6SE
(0171 421 6800)

Office of Her Majesty's Chief Inspector (Wales) (OHMCI)
Phase 1 Government Buildings
Ty Glas, Llanishen
Cardiff CF4 5FQ (01222 761456)

School Curriculum and Assessment Authority (SCAA)
Newcombe House
45 Notting Hill Gate
London W11 3JB
(0171 229 1234)

Funding Agency for Schools
25 Skeldergate
York YO1 2XL (01904 661661)

Welsh Funding Council
Lambourne House
Cardiff Business Park, Llanishen
Cardiff CF4 5GL (01222 761861)

Local government

Assocation of London Government
36 Old Queen Street
London SW1H 9JF (0171 222 7799)

Association of County Councils
Eaton House
66A Eaton Square
London SW1W 9BH
(0171 235 1200)

Association of District Councils
26 Chapter Street
London SW1P 4ND
(0171 233 6868)

Association of Metropolitan Authorities
35 Great Smith Street
London SW1P 3JB
(0171 222 8100)

Note: The three above local government associations are amalgamating in April 1997 and will be known as
Local Government Association
Eaton House
66A Eaton Square
London SW1 9BH
(0171 235 1200)

Useful Organisations

Governors' organisations

Action for Governors Information and Training (AGIT)
Lyng Hall
Blackberry Lane
Coventry CV2 3JS
(01203 63679)

Institute of School and College Governors (ISCG)
Avondale Park School
Sirdar Road
London W11 4EE
(Helpline 0171 229 0200)

National Association of Governors and Managers (NAGM)
21 Bennetts Hill
Birmingham B2 5QP
(0121 643 5787) (Helpline 0800 241242)

National Governors' Council
Glebe House
Church Street
Crediton
Devon EX17 2AF
(Helpline 01363 774377)

Others

Advisory Centre for Education (ACE)
1B Aberdeen Studios
22 Highbury Grove
London N5 2DQ (0171 354 8318) (Helpline 0171 554 8321)

Campaign for State Education (CASE)
158 Durham Road
London SW20 0DG
(0181 944 8206)

Grant Maintained Schools Foundation
36 Great Smith Street
London SW1P 3BU (0171 233 4666)

Local Schools Information (LSI)
2nd floor, 1-5 Bath Street
London EC1V 9QQ
(0171 490 4942)

Further Reading

(for addresses see useful organisations)

ACE Bulletin (bi-monthly), ACE

ACE Governors' Handbook, 3rd ed, 1995, ACE

AGIT Do-It-Better Guides, packs of 15 copies 1995 to date, AGIT

Basics for Schools Governors by Joan Sallis, 1993, AGIT

The Collected Governors Guides, 1995, AGIT

County and Voluntary Schools: spot the difference by Jane Arden, 1995, AGIT

Effective Governors for Effective Schools ed Derek Esp and Rene Saran, 1995, Pitman Publishing

The Good School Governor : in a nutshell by Joan Sallis, 1994, AGIT

Governors' Action (5 issues a year), AGIT

Governors' News (4 issues a year) and NAGM Papers on a variety of subjects), NAGM

Guidance on a Minimum Entitlement for School Governors, 1996, AGIT

Heads and Governors: building the partnership by Joan Sallis, 1995, AGIT

How Schools Work: a really simple guide for governors and parents, by Joan Sallis, 1995, ACE

Manual for Clerks of Governing Bodies, 1995, ISCG

Lessons in Teamwork, 1995, Audit Commission/OFSTED, HMSO

Moving to Management: school governors in the 1990s, by Angela Thody 1992, David Fulton

Parent Governors: your own guide by Joan Sallis, 1995, Northants County Council, Governor Services, Russell House, Rickyard Road, The Arbours, Northampton

School Governors: a guide to the law in four versions to cover
1. County controlled and special agreement schools
2. Aided schools
3. Special schools
4. Grant maintained schools, 1994, free from DfEE Publications Centre, PO Box 6927, London E3

continued on p.46

Further Reading

3NZ (0171 510 0150)
School Governing Bodies: Making Progress by Peter Earley, 1995, NFER, The Mere, Upton Park, Slough, Berks SL1 2DQ
School Governors: a question and answer guide by Joan Sallis, 1995, Butterworth Heinemann/AGIT

School Governors: leaders or followers? ed Angela Thody, 1994, Longman

Stop Press: monthly news digest for Governors, AGIT

Teacher Governors: your own guide by Joan Sallis, 1996, Northants County Council

Working Together; rules and good practice for school governors by Joan Sallis, 1993. Northants County Council (as above

How Schools Work

a really simple guide for governors and parents

Parents are being offered more of a say in schools but for new governors and parents, in particular, the changes in organisation, curriculum and classroom practice make schools bewildering places. This guide by **Joan Sallis**, the author of this book and herself a long-standing governor of a comprehensive school, explains who does what, where funding comes from and how parents can get involved. 1995
£5.00 + £1.00 p&p
Available from the Advisory Centre for Education,
1B Aberdeen Studios, 22,Highbury Grove, London N5 2DQ